Happy Valentine's Day

Recipes

Make the Day Special with Delicious Meals & Treats!

BY: Allie Allen

COOK & ENJOY

Copyright 2021 Allie Allen

Copyright Notes

This book is written as an informational tool. While the author has taken every precaution to ensure the accuracy of the information provided therein, the reader is warned that they assume all risk when following the content. The author will not be held responsible for any damages that may occur as a result of the readers' actions.

The author does not give permission to reproduce this book in any form, including but not limited to: print, social media posts, electronic copies or photocopies, unless permission is expressly given in writing.

Table of Contents

Introduction

What kinds of dishes have the most bang for your buck in the love department?

What ingredients will help to make Valentine's Day more romantic?

Are the ingredients easy to find?

There are many more ingredients that play well into your hands when you're making a dish that could help dinner lead to intimacy. Chocolate and strawberries have been savored for years by people in love. The chocolate makes you feel good, and strawberries are SO romantic since they're juicy, sweet and shaped like hearts!

Caffeine, included with coffee, cream, milk and mocha allows the heat of a drink to melt someone's heart. Caffeine can also speed up heart rate and make you more alert to signals that your special one feels romantic.

Pomegranates, in berry form or juice, are sweet and packed with antioxidants that increase your blood flow. They can ease stress and allow you to be more relaxed with your date.

Spaghetti is a bit messy for a date, but Italian food like pasta has carbs that give you the energy to burn. Pasta helps you to achieve an elegant meal with a relatively simple recipe.

From peppers to strawberries, the romantic food can help set the tone for a memorable Valentine's Day. Turn the page and let's get cooking…

Valentine's Day Breakfast Recipes...

1 – Nutella & Strawberry Crepes

These French crepes made the authentic way are the perfect Valentine's Day breakfast. The Nutella nut spread and tasty strawberries add a wonderful final touch.

Makes 10 Servings

Cooking + Prep Time: 50 minutes + 3 hours chilling time

Ingredients:

- 2 tbsp. of melted butter, unsalted
- 2 eggs, large
- 1/2 cup of water, filtered
- 3/4 cup of milk, whole
- 1 cup of flour, all-purpose
- 2 tbsp. of sugar, granulated
- For griddle: 4-6 tbsp. butter, unsalted
- 1/2 cup of Nutella nut spread

Instructions:

Mix water, eggs, butter, milk, sugar and flour together in food processor. Blend & pulse for one minute or so, mixing completely.

Cover food processor. Allow mixture to settle for 10 minutes or more. Sit mixture in the refrigerator for several hours, to chill.

Heat non-stick pan over med-high heat. Use butter to coat. Be sure heat isn't too high – otherwise the butter may get too brown, or burn.

Pour 1/8 cup of batter into pan. Swirl and spread batter thinly. Cook for 1/2 minute or so.

Flip the crepe. Be careful, as they are delicate and thin.

Allow crepe to cook for 10 more seconds. It should be yellow in color with several brown marks and spots. Remove crepe from heat. Repeat till you have used all the batter.

Spread nut spread over crepes. Fold in fourths. Add strawberries on top and serve.

2 – Miniature Omelet Muffins

These mini omelet muffins are easy to bake and the perfect Valentine's Day morning treat. Their recipe uses favorite ingredients for omelets, but you can substitute which way you'd like.

Makes 6 Servings

Cooking + Prep Time: 35 minutes

Ingredients:

- Cooking spray, non-stick
- 9 eggs, large
- 1/4 tsp. of salt, kosher
- Pepper, black
- 3 strips of bacon, cooked and chopped
- 3 tbsp. of frozen, thawed, drained spinach
- 3 tbsp. of tomatoes, diced
- 3 tbsp. of onion, diced
- 3 tbsp. of bell pepper, diced
- 2 oz. of cheddar cheese shreds

Instructions:

Preheat oven to 350 degrees F. Then, use non-stick spray to spray muffin pans.

Whisk eggs in large mixing bowl. Season as desired. Add remainder of ingredients and mix well.

Fill muffin tins. Place on cookie sheet. Then, bake in 350F oven for 20-25 minutes or so, till the muffins have set. Serve.

3 – Decadent Chocolate & Ice Cream Waffles

This chocolate waffle recipe is a great reason to utilize your waffle maker. They can be made easily, and they have the chocolate everyone loves on Valentine's Day.

Makes 6 Servings

Cooking + Prep Time: 1/2 hour

Ingredients:

- 1 & 3/4 cups of flour, all-purpose
- 6 tbsp. of sugar, granulated
- 4 tsp. of baking powder
- 2 eggs, large
- 1/2 tsp. of salt, kosher
- 1 cup of milk, whole
- 3 tbsp. of shortening, vegetable
- 2 oz. of chocolate chips, semi-sweet
- Cooking spray
- To serve: chocolate sauce, ice cream, cocoa powder

Instructions:

In large-sized bowl, combine the flour, baking powder, sugar & kosher salt.

In separate bowl, whisk milk & eggs together.

Add egg & milk mixture to flour mixture. Stir and combine well.

Melt chocolate and shortening in glass bowl over small pot of water at a simmer.

Stir the chocolate mixture in waffle batter.

Preheat waffle iron. Coat using non-stick spray or brush with some butter, so the waffles won't stick.

Spoon batter in heated waffle iron. Spread it out. Close lid & cook till waffles are done as you prefer. Repeat with remainder of batter.

Dust the waffles using cocoa powder and serve.

4 – Cinnamon & Cream Cheese Pancakes

Pancakes are a favorite breakfast anytime, and these are special for your special one. They're classic pancakes with cinnamon & cream cheese flavors.

Makes 16 Servings

Cooking + Prep Time: 1/2 hour

Ingredients:

For the cinnamon filling:

- 8 tbsp. of melted butter, unsalted
- 1/2 cup + 2 tbsp. of brown sugar, light, packed
- 1 tbsp. of cinnamon, ground

For the cream cheese flavored glaze:

- 8 tbsp. of butter, unsalted
- 4 oz. of room temp. cream cheese, light
- 1 & 1/2 cups of sugar, powdered
- 1 tsp. of vanilla extract, pure

For the pancakes:

- 2 cups of flour, all-purpose
- 4 tsp. of baking powder
- 1 tsp. of salt, kosher
- 2 cups of milk, 2%
- 2 lightly beaten eggs, large
- 2 tbsp. of oil, vegetable or canola

Instructions:

To prepare the filling, stir together butter, cinnamon and brown sugar in medium mixing bowl.

Add the mixture to a zipper top freezer bag.

Snip corner of bag. Squeeze filling into that corner. Set filling aside.

To prepare glaze, melt butter in small-sized pan on low heat. Remove pan from the heat. Whisk in cream cheese till smooth.

Add powdered sugar slowly, while stirring.

Add vanilla and stir again. Set glaze aside.

To prepare pancakes, whisk together the flour, salt and baking powder.

Add and whisk the milk, oil and eggs and mix till batter has moistened.

Heat skillet. Spray using cooking spray.

Scoop 3/4 cup of pancake batter into skillet. Make a 4" diameter circle.

When pancake begins bubbling, add cinnamon filling by squeezing from bag in circular swirls.

Cook pancake till bottom has turned a golden brown. Flip it and cook for a couple minutes on second side, till it is golden brown, too. Repeat with remainder of batter.

Rewarm glaze if needed. Drizzle glaze over pancakes and serve.

5 – Heart-Egg Toast

This simple heart-shaped egg toast covers all the bases for breakfast. A cookie cutter makes it easy to cut into heart shapes.

Makes 1 Serving

Cooking + Prep Time: 5-7 minutes

Ingredients:

- 1 slice of toasted bread, whole-wheat
- 1 tbsp. of butter, unsalted
- 1 egg, large
- Salt, kosher, as desired
- Pepper, black, as desired

Instructions:

Use a cookie cutter in a heart shape to stamp out middle of bread.

Heat pan on med. heat. Add melted butter and swirl, coating pan.

Add bread to pan. Cook till first side is golden brown. Flip over and crack egg into hole in bread. Reduce heat level to low. Cover pan. Cook for two minutes, till egg cooks through.

Toast cut out piece of bread too, to dip in egg. Season as desired. Serve.

Valentine's Day Lunch, Dinner, Side Dish and Appetizer Recipes...

6 – Red Valentine's Day Chili

Fire roasted ripe tomatoes and beets give this hearty chili a Valentine's Day color. You can actually serve it anytime.

Makes 6 Servings

Cooking + Prep Time: 1 hour & 35 minutes

Ingredients:

- 2 tsp. of cumin, ground
- 1 tsp. of oregano, dried
- 1/2 tsp. of chili powder, chipotle
- 2 tbsp. of oil, vegetable
- 3 beets, large
- 1 red pepper, large
- Pepper, ground, as desired
- 4 garlic cloves
- 1 can of tomatoes, diced, fire-roasted
- 1 & 1/2 cups of black beans, cooked
- 1 & 1/2 cups of kidney beans, red, cooked
- 1 & 1/2 cups of pinto beans, cooked
- 1 cup of water, filtered
- 1 cup of sour cream, reduced fat
- 1/4 cup of cilantro leaves, fresh

Instructions:

In large pot, combine oregano, chili powder and cumin. Cook on med. heat for one to two minutes, till fragrant and toasted. Transfer mixture to wax paper and set it aside.

In same pot, heat the oil over med. heat till hot. Add the peppers, onions, beets & black pepper as desired. Cook while stirring occasionally for 15-17 minutes till veggies become tender.

Add spice mixture from step 1, along with garlic, to pot. Cook while constantly stirring for two minutes. Add the water, tomatoes and beans. Heat over med-high till boiling.

Reduce the heat level to med-low. Simmer for 1/2 hour, occasionally mashing and stirring some of the beans. Season as desired. Divide in bowls. Use sour cream & cilantro to top. Serve.

7 – Roasted Pepper Soup

This soup is so creamy; it's a favorite in our home. It warms you up on a chilly Valentine's Day or any cold-weather day.

Makes 4 Servings

Cooking + Prep Time: 35 minutes

Ingredients:

- 2 tbsp. of oil, olive
- 1 chopped onion, large
- 4 smashed garlic cloves
- Salt, kosher, as desired
- Pepper, ground, as desired
- 1 tsp. of coriander, ground
- 2 x 12-oz. jars of drained, chopped red peppers, roasted
- 1 x 15-oz. can of rinsed chickpeas
- 1 x 32-oz. can of broth, veggie or chicken, low sodium
- 2 tbsp. of vinegar, sherry
- To serve: chopped cilantro, sliced almonds &/or sliced green onions

Instructions:

Heat a large-sized Dutch oven over med. heat. Add oil, garlic & onions. Season as desired. Cover while it cooks for five minutes, while occasionally stirring.

Uncover the Dutch oven. Add coriander and stir. Cook for one minute. Add broth, red peppers and chickpeas. Cover. Bring to boil. Allow to boil for five minutes or so. Remove pan from the heat. Add vinegar and stir.

Use an immersion blender to puree soup till you have a smooth texture. Top with cilantro, almonds &/or green onions, as desired. Serve.

8 – Smoked Steak & Lentils

Steak is a common choice for Valentine's Day dinner. However, this recipe utilizes different combinations of spices that make it unique.

Makes 4 Servings

Cooking + Prep Time: 35 minutes

Ingredients:

- 3 tbsp. of oil, olive
- 1 finely chopped garlic clove
- 1 cup of lentils, dry
- 1/4 cup of white wine, dry
- 3 cups of chicken broth, low sodium
- 2 x 1"-thick steak strips
- 1 tbsp. of paprika, smoked + extra for garnish
- Salt, kosher, as desired
- Pepper, ground, as desired
- 1 x 5-oz. pkg. of spinach, baby
- To serve: chopped parsley & Greek yogurt

Instructions:

First, in med. pan, heat a tbsp. of oil and the garlic over med. heat till garlic edges are sizzling. Add the lentils. Toss, coating well. Add the wine. Simmer for two minutes.

Add the broth. Cover pan partially & bring to boil. Reduce the heat. Simmer till tender, 18-22 minutes.

Next, use paper towels to pat the steaks dry. Rub with paprika and season as desired.

Heat a tbsp. of oil in large-sized skillet over med. heat. Then, cook steaks to your preferred level of doneness. Transfer to cutting board. Allow to rest for 5-10 minutes, then slice.

Discard excess liquid from the lentils. Fold in the last tbsp. of oil, along with spinach. Season as desired. Use yogurt dollop and parsley & paprika sprinkled, as desired. Serve.

9 – Seafood Paella

This dish includes some of the sea's tastiest offerings, shrimp, clams & squid. It's a fancy looking dinner, but easy to prepare.

Makes 6 Servings

Cooking + Prep Time: 1 hour & 15 minutes

Ingredients:

- 1/3 cup of oil, olive
- 8 oz. of shrimp, deveined, shelled
- 8 oz. of rinsed, patted dry, sliced squid bodies
- 1 finely chopped onion, medium
- 1 x 14-oz. can of diced, drained tomatoes, fire-roasted
- 3 chopped garlic cloves
- 1 & 1/2 cups of rice, Arborio
- 3 & 1/2 cups of broth, seafood
- 1 x 8-oz. bottle of juice, clam
- 12 scrubbed clams, littleneck
- For garnishing: lemon wedges and parsley

Instructions:

In a deep, heavy skillet, heat the oil over med-high till hot. Don't let it smoke. Add the squid, shrimp and a pinch of kosher salt. Cook for two minutes, stirring one time, till shrimp begin browning. Transfer them to med-sized bowl.

Reduce the heat level to med. Add tomatoes & onions. Cook while stirring frequently for eight to nine minutes. Add the garlic and cook for two minutes. Add the rice. Stir while cooking for two minutes.

Add clam juice and broth to the skillet. Stir so that the rice is evenly distributed. Heat over med-high till boiling. Allow to boil for 12-15 minutes while not stirring.

Nestle the clams, shrimp and squid over rice. Cover the skillet. Cook for 10-15 minutes more, till rice turns tender and clams have opened. Remove skillet from the heat. Cover and allow to stand for 10-12 minutes. Garnish with lemons & parsley and serve.

10 – Tilapia & Zoodles

Tilapia is not a common choice for dinner on Valentine's day, but it is light and delicate. That way, you can save room for a scrumptious dessert.

Makes 4 Servings

Cooking + Prep Time: 1/2 hour

Ingredients:

- 1 & 1/2 pounds of zucchini
- 3 tbsp. of oil, olive
- Salt, kosher, as desired
- Pepper, ground, as desired
- 4 tilapia fillets, small
- 1 thinly sliced lemon, fresh
- 2 thinly sliced garlic cloves
- 1/2 cup of chopped parsley, flat leaf
- 1 tbsp. of capers

Instructions:

Heat the oven to 475F. Use foil to line large, rimmed cookie sheet. Then, use a spiralizer or vegetable peeler to slice the zucchini into ribbons known as zoodles.

Transfer zoodles to cookie sheet. Toss with 1 tbsp. of oil. Season as desired. Roast for 12-15 minutes. Raise heat up to broil. Continue cooking till zoodles turn golden brown, three to four minutes.

Heat 1 tbsp. of oil in large, heavy skillet on med-high. Season the tilapia as desired. Cook till the fish is opaque, two to three minutes each side. Transfer fish to plates.

Add last tbsp. of oil to skillet, with capers, lemon and garlic. Stir occasionally while cooking till garlic is tender and golden-brown. Toss with the parsley. Spoon over the tilapia. Serve along with zucchini.

11 – Grilled Eggplant & Tomato Salad

This colorful meal will brighten your table with its veggies and other ingredients. It includes creamy and cool yogurt, smoky eggplants and fresh tomatoes.

Makes 6 Servings

Cooking + Prep Time: 35 minutes

Ingredients:

- 2 x 1/2"-thick sliced eggplants, medium, 1 lb. each +/-
- 1/4 cup + 3 tbsp. of oil, olive
- 1 tsp. of coriander, ground
- 1 tsp. of ground pepper, cayenne
- 1/4 cup of chopped mint leaves, fresh, + extra for garnishing
- 3 chopped small chilies, red Fresno or other hot type
- 2 tbsp. of lemon juice, fresh
- 2 tbsp. of vinegar, red wine
- 1 & 1/2 cups of halved grape or cherry tomatoes
- 1/4 cup of yogurt, Greek
- 2 tbsp. of milk, whole

Instructions:

Heat the grill to medium. Brush whole eggplants with 1/4 cup of oil. Then, sprinkle using 1/4 tsp. of salt, coriander and cayenne. Grill till tender, 10-12 minutes.

In medium mixing bowl, whisk together the lemon juice, chilies, mint, vinegar, 1/2 tsp. of salt & last 3 tbsp. of oil till combined well. To this dressing, add the tomatoes and toss, combining thoroughly.

In small-sized bowl, stir milk and yogurt together.

Arrange the eggplants on large platter. Top with the dressing. Drizzle over the top with milk & yogurt mixture. Use extra mint leaves to garnish, if you like. Serve.

12 – Salmon & Lentil-Lemon Salad

This easy recipe takes less than a half-hour to prepare. Salmon is a healthy and light option for dinner that still makes Valentine's Day special.

Makes 4 Servings

Cooking + Prep Time: 25 minutes

Ingredients:

- 4 x 5-oz. salmon fillets, skinless
- 2 tbsp. + 2 tsp. of oil, olive
- 2 halved lemons, fresh
- 2 tsp. of mustard, Dijon
- 1 tsp. of thyme, fresh
- 1/2 finely chopped small onion, red
- 1 x 15-oz. can of rinsed lentils
- 1 chunk-cut small cucumber, seedless
- 4 cups of spinach, baby
- 1/4 cup of roughly chopped dill, fresh
- 1/4 tsp. of salt, kosher
- 1/4 tsp. of pepper, ground

Instructions:

Heat a large-sized skillet over medium heat.

Season salmon fillets using 1/4 tsp. of salt and 1/4 tsp. of ground pepper. Add 2 tsp. of oil to the skillet. Then, add the salmon & 2 lemon halves with the cut sides facing down. Cook for five minutes each side, till salmon turns fully opaque. Squeeze halved lemons over the salmon.

In large-sized bowl, whisk juice from second halved lemon, along with last 2 tbsp. of oil and mustard. Season as desired. Stir in the fresh thyme. Toss with lentils and onions. Fold in the spinach, dill and cucumbers. Serve salad with cooked salmon.

13 – Thai Lettuce Wraps

These turkey and lettuce wraps are healthy and easy to make. The lime juice and mint flavor them nicely, and the squirt of hot sriracha gives them a kick.

Makes 4 Servings

Cooking + Prep Time: 25 minutes

Ingredients:

- 2 seeded, chopped bell peppers, medium
- 1 tbsp. of oil, vegetable
- 3 chopped garlic cloves
- 1 pound of turkey, ground
- 2 tbsp. of fish sauce, low sodium
- 1/4 cup of chopped cilantro, fresh
- 1/4 cup of chopped mint leaves, fresh
- 3 tbsp. of lime juice, fresh
- 1/2 tsp. of sugar, granulated
- To serve: sriracha sauce & lettuce cups

Instructions:

To skillet over med-high heat, add vegetable oil. Cook the bell peppers for three minutes. Add the garlic and cook for 1/2 minute. Add turkey & fish sauce and cook for five minutes, as you break up the meat.

Stir in lime juice, sugar, mint leaves and cilantro. Add to lettuce cups and drizzle with hot sauce, as desired. Serve.

14 – Seared Chops & Cherries

This special dinner doesn't take long to prepare. The cherries add a unique flavor and a red color for Valentine's Day.

Makes 4 Servings

Cooking + Prep Time: 40 minutes

Ingredients:

- 1 tbsp. of oil, olive
- 4 x 6-oz. pork chops, boneless
- Salt, kosher, as desired
- Pepper, ground, as desired
- 1 cup of pitted, halved cherries
- 1/4 cup of white wine, dry
- 2 tsp. of mustard, whole-grain
- 2 bunches of spinach – trim the tough stems

Instructions:

Heat the oil in large-sized skillet over medium heat. Then, pat the pork chops dry using paper towels. Season as desired. Cook for 8-10 minutes each side till barely cooked through and golden brown. Transfer them to dinner plates.

Add the cherries to your skillet. Stir occasionally while cooking for about two minutes, till they start softening. Add the wine. Cook for about two more minutes, till wine has been reduced to one tablespoon or so.

Stir in 1/3 cup water, mustard and spinach. Toss while cooking for one to two minutes, till spinach begins wilting. Serve with the pork.

15 – Shrimp & Vegetable Ziti

Your Valentine never needs to know how simple this dish is prepared. The shrimp and veggies round out the pasta dish for a special dinner.

Makes 6 Servings

Cooking + Prep Time: 30 minutes

Ingredients:

- 1 pound of ziti – you can substitute rigatoni if you prefer
- 3 garlic cloves
- 1 x 14 & 1/2-oz. can of tomatoes, crushed
- 2/3 cup of half 'n half
- 1 pound of shrimp, peeled & deveined
- 1 cup of peas, frozen

Instructions:

Cook the pasta using the directions on package.

To prepare the sauce, chop the cloves of garlic. Add to deep skillet along with 3 tbsp. of oil. Cook and stir over medium heat for three minutes.

Add the tomatoes & half 'n half to the skillet. Heat till it simmers, and stir while it continues simmering, for two minutes.

Add the shrimp and peas to skillet. Season as desired. Cook for about five minutes, till shrimp have cooked fully. Serve pasta, shrimp & veggies with sauce.

16 – Red Wine & Beef

Indeed, you don't need to plan much in advance to prepare this flavorful and rich dish. It's a perfect Valentine's Day dinner.

Makes 4 Servings

Cooking + Prep Time: 25 minutes + 4-5 hours slow cooker time

Ingredients:

- 1 can of tomatoes, crushed
- 1/2 cup of wine, red
- Salt, kosher, as desired
- Pepper, ground, as desired
- 1 can of tomatoes, peeled, whole
- 4 garlic cloves
- 2 carrots, medium
- 1 onion, large
- 2 sprigs of rosemary, fresh
- 1 & 1/2 pounds of stew meat, beef, lean
- 12 oz. of noodles, wide
- 1/2 cup of chopped parsley, flat-leaf, fresh
- 1/4 cup of Parmesan cheese, grated

Instructions:

In a slow cooker, whisk red wine and crushed tomatoes together. Season as desired. Add whole tomatoes and break them into piece using your hands. Add and stir in carrots, garlic, rosemary and onions.

Add stew meat. Coat by turning. Cover slow cooker. Then, cook for four to five hours on the high setting, till beef has cooked fully through and will shred easily.

20 minutes before you're ready to eat, cook pasta using instructions on package.

Remove rosemary from slow cooker. Skim off fat, if any rises to top. Break meat into small pieces with a fork. Stir them into cooking liquid and fold in parsley.

Ladle beef ragu atop pasta. Use Parmesan cheese for sprinkling and serve.

17 – Herb & Lemon Roast Chicken

This is a classic recipe for roast chicken that will be appreciated on Valentine's Day. It is subtly added to with the notes of thyme and citrus.

Makes 6 Servings

Cooking + Prep Time: 1 & 1/2 hours

Ingredients:

For the roast chicken:

- 2 tsp. of lemon zest, grated finely
- 2 crushed garlic cloves
- 1 tsp. of chopped thyme, fresh
- 4 tbsp. of unsalted butter, softened
- 1 x 4-5-pound chicken, whole

For roasted vegetables:

- 1 thinly sliced onion, medium
- 1 bunch of trimmed and quartered radishes

Instructions:

Preheat the oven to 350F.

In a medium bowl, mash 2 tbsp. of butter, thyme, garlic and zest till combined well. Season as desired.

Peel skin from chicken thighs and breast gently with your fingers. Place butter mixture under the skin and evenly spread it. Tie the drumsticks together. Tuck the wings behind the breast.

Fit a rack into medium-sized roasting pan. Place chicken on the rack. Arrange radishes and onions around it.

Melt last 2 tbsp. of butter and brush it over the chicken. Season as desired. Add 1/4 cup of water to bottom of the roasting pan.

Roast the chicken in 350F oven for 45-50 minutes. Adjust temperature of oven to 425F.

Continue roasting chicken and check periodically to be sure all water has not evaporated. Add extra water as needed. Roast for 15-20 minutes, till meat thermometer in thigh reads 165F.

Remove chicken from pan and allow it to rest for 15-20 minutes before you carve it. Serve with the vegetable and butter mixture.

18 – Broccoli & Chicken Bow Tie Pasta

This simple pasta recipe is so tasty, it's sure to please even the pickiest eaters. It's a solid meal, and plenty special enough for Valentine's Day.

Makes 4 Servings

Cooking + Prep Time: 25 minutes

Ingredients:

- 2 cups of floret-cut broccoli
- Salt, kosher, as desired
- Pepper, ground, as desired
- 1 bunch of basil, fresh
- 2 garlic cloves
- 1/4 cup of oil, olive
- 2 tsp. of lemon zest, fresh
- 3 oz. of Parmesan cheese
- 4 oz. of cream cheese, light
- 2 cups of rotisserie chicken, shredded

Instructions:

Cook broccoli in salted, boiling water for five minutes or so, till tender. Remove to medium bowl. Add the pasta to boiling water. Cook using instructions on package, then drain.

Process the oil, garlic, basil, red pepper, lemon zest & Parmesan cheese in food processor till chopped finely. Add the broccoli. Pulse four to six times, till chopped coarsely. Season as desired.

Stir cream cheese and broccoli pesto into the pasta till coated well, then fold in the chicken and coat. Serve.

19 – Zucchini Shrimp Scampi

Pasta dinners aren't always heavy. This zucchini and shrimp scampi dish is light, using the sauce made with white wine.

Makes 6 Servings

Cooking + Prep Time: 20 minutes

Ingredients:

- 1 & 1/2 pounds of shrimp, shelled & deveined
- 2 tbsp. of oil, olive
- 2 sliced zucchinis, medium
- 4 chopped garlic cloves
- 4 tbsp. of butter, unsalted
- 3/4 cup of wine, white
- 1/8 tsp. of salt, kosher
- 1 pound of cooked linguine
- 1/4 cup of cooking water from pasta
- 2 tsp. of grated lemon peel, fresh
- To serve: fresh parsley, chopped

Instructions:

Prepare pasta using instructions on package and drain. Reserve 1/4 cup of the cooking water.

Cook the shrimp in olive oil in skillet, turning once, till cooked through, about three minutes. Transfer the shrimp to a plate.

Add butter, zucchini and garlic to the skillet and cook for three minutes. Add the wine & salt and cook for two minutes, while scraping and stirring.

Toss the vegetables with the shrimp and linguine, cooking water from pasta, parsley and lemon peel. Serve.

Valentine's Day Dessert Recipes...

20 – Velvety Valentine Cookies

This cut-out cookie treat is delicious and rich, perfect for Valentine's Day or other special occasions. It's easy to make and SO tasty!

Makes 24 Servings

Cooking + Prep Time: 25 minutes

Ingredients:

- 1/2 lb. of softened butter, unsalted
- 2 & 1/2 cups of sifted flour, all-purpose
- 1 cup of sifted sugar, powdered
- 1 tbsp. of milk, whole or 2%
- 1 tsp. of vanilla extract, pure

Instructions:

Preheat the oven to 325F.

Mix the butter in mixer till it's light, and add the rest of the ingredients.

Knead the dough till it has a velvety texture.

Roll 1/2 of dough after another to 1/4" thickness. Use just a bit of flour to assist you.

Cut out the cookies. Bake on greased cookie sheet in 325F oven for 12-13 minutes. The cookies are done when almost white. Serve.

21 – Raspberry & White Chocolate Thins

These crispy cookies are drizzled with decadent white chocolate, making them a perfect Valentine's Day treat. They are topped with crushed raspberries for an elegant touch.

Makes 2 to 4 dozen Servings

Cooking + Prep Time: 45 minutes + 20 minutes freezing time

Ingredients:

- 2 & 1/2 cups of raspberries, freeze-dried
- 2 & 1/2 cups of flour, all-purpose
- 1/4 tsp. of salt, kosher
- 1/2 tsp. of baking powder
- 2 sticks of room temperature butter, unsalted
- 3/4 cup of sugar, granulated
- 1 egg, large
- 1 & 1/2 tsp. of vanilla extract, pure
- To drizzle: white chocolate, melted

Instructions:

In a food processor, grind raspberries finely.

In large mixing bowl, whisk powdered raspberries, baking powder, flour & kosher salt together.

Next, in separate bowl, use an electric mixer to beat the butter & sugar together for three minutes or so, till fluffy and light. Beat in the egg, then the vanilla extract.

Reduce mixer to low speed. Add flour mixture gradually, mixing only till barely incorporated. Shape the dough in 2 x 2" square logs. Use cling wrap to wrap the logs and freeze them for 20-25 minutes.

Then, heat the oven to 350F. Line two cookie sheets with baking paper. Slice the dough in 1/8" thick squares and place them on cookie sheets.

Bake in 350F oven for 10-12 minutes and rotate when halfway done, till cookies have golden brown edges. Then, allow them to cool for about five minutes and transfer onto racks and allow to finish cooling.

Drizzle the cookies using melted chocolate. Sprinkle the tops with crushed raspberries. Serve.

22 – Red Velvet Valentine Cupcakes

Everyone seems to love red velvet cake, and these cupcakes made the same way are a wonderful Valentine's Day treat. They are gorgeously colored, moist and not overly sweet.

Makes 12 Servings

Cooking + Prep Time: 1 hour & 5 minutes

Ingredients:

Dry:

- 1 & 1/3 cups of flour, all-purpose
- 3 tbsp. of cocoa powder, unsweetened
- 1 tsp. of baking powder
- 1/2 tsp. of salt, kosher
- 1/4 tsp. of baking soda

Wet:

- 1/4 cup of softened butter, unsalted
- 1 cup of sugar, granulated
- 2 eggs, large
- 3/4 cup of buttermilk, low-fat
- 2 tsp. of vinegar, white
- 1 tsp. of vanilla extract
- 1 tbsp. of food coloring, red

Instructions:

Preheat the oven to 350F. Line 12 cups of muffin tin using paper liners.

In large sized mixing bowl, sift the flour, cocoa, kosher salt, baking powder & baking soda together till combined well.

Place unsalted butter & granulated sugar in bowl of stand mixer w/whisk attachment affixed. Beat them together till fluffy and light. Add eggs into this mixture, one after another. Mix first one in well before you add second.

Beat the buttermilk & vinegar into the moist mixture. Add vanilla extract, then food coloring. Mix till you have an even color.

Pour dry ingredients in wet mixture. Hand-whisk till you have a smooth batter. Spoon it into muffin cups, about 3/4 of the way full.

Bake cupcakes in 350F oven for 20-25 minutes, till you can insert a toothpick in middle of a cupcake and have it come back clean. Allow to sit in pan for 10-12 minutes.

Remove cupcakes from the pan. Then, allow to cool on wire rack. Unwrap and frost. Serve.

23 – Chocolate Valentine's Day Mug Cake

Baking for Valentine's Day doesn't always mean making something fancy. This individual cake cooks in a mug in the microwave in just a few minutes!

Makes 1 Serving

Cooking + Prep Time: 5 minutes

Ingredients:

- 1/4 cup of flour, all-purpose
- 2 tbsp. of sugar, granulated
- 2 tbsp. of cocoa powder, unsweetened
- 1/4 tsp. of baking powder
- 1/8 tsp. of salt, kosher
- 1/3 cup of milk, whole
- 2 tbsp. of melted butter, unsalted
- 2 tsp. of vanilla extract, pure
- 4 quartered squares of caramel
- 1/4 cup of chopped pecans, toasted

Instructions:

In 12-oz. microwave-safe mug, whisk sugar, flour, baking powder, cocoa powder & salt together. Stir in the milk, vanilla and butter. Fold in the pecans and caramel.

Microwave on the high setting for 90 seconds or so, till barely cooked through. Serve.

24 – Strawberry & Pretzels Dessert

This is a special dessert that is sweet and salty, both. It's especially decorative when you make it in a clear casserole dish.

Makes 12 Servings

Cooking + Prep Time: 50 minutes + chilling time

Ingredients:

- 2 cups of pretzels, crushed
- 3/4 cup of melted butter, unsalted
- 3 tbsp. of sugar, granulated
- 1 x 8-oz. pkg. of softened cream cheese, light
- 1 cup of sugar, granulated
- 1 x 8-oz. container of frozen and thawed whipped topping
- 2 x 3-oz. pkgs. of gelatin, strawberry flavor
- 2 cups of water, boiling
- 2 x 10-oz. pkgs. of strawberries, frozen

Instructions:

Preheat the oven to 400F.

Stir butter, pretzels & 3 tbsp. of sugar together. Combine well. Press in bottom of 13" x 9" casserole dish. A clear dish is best.

Bake in 400F oven till set, 8-10 minutes. Set dish aside and allow it to cool.

In large-sized bowl, combine cream cheese with 1 cup of sugar. Fold in the whipped topping. Spread onto crust.

Dissolve the gelatin in boiling, filtered water. Stir in frozen strawberries. Allow to briefly set. When the mixture has the consistency of egg whites +/-, pour, then spread over the cream cheese. Place in refrigerator till dessert sets. Serve.

25 – Cinnamon & Sugar Churros

Want an original treat for Valentine's Day? These churros are crispy outside and fluffy inside, and you must also make the caramel-chocolate dipping sauce for a wonderful finishing touch.

Makes 24 Servings

Cooking + Prep Time: 35 minutes

Ingredients:

For sauce:

- 1/2 cup of sugar, granulated
- 4 tbsp. of cut up butter pieces, unsalted
- 1/2 cup of room temperature cream, heavy
- 2 oz. of cocoa powder, unsweetened
- A pinch of salt, kosher
- 2 oz. of chopped chocolate, dark

For churros:

- 1 stick of cinnamon
- 1/4 cup of oil, olive
- 1 tbsp. + 1/2 cup of sugar, granulated
- 1/2 tsp. of salt, kosher
- 1 cup of flour, all-purpose
- For frying: oil, vegetable
- 1 egg, large
- 1/2 tsp. of cinnamon, ground

Instructions:

To prepare the sauce, combine 2 tbsp. of water and sugar with a fork in small pan. Cook over med. heat and swirl as needed for four to five minutes, till mixture is the color of amber.

Remove pan from the heat. Expect sputtering as you whisk in the butter. Whisk in cream, salt & cocoa powder. Add the chocolate. Allow mixture to set for three minutes. Stir till smooth and melted.

To prepare the churros, in medium pan, cook the stick of cinnamon over med. heat for two minutes or so, till fragrant. Add 1 cup of water, oil, 1 tbsp. of sugar & kosher salt. Bring to boil. Discard stick of cinnamon and remove pan from heat. Stir in flour quickly. Allow to set.

Fill medium pan with four inches of oil. Heat over med. heat till candy thermometer reads 350F.

Transfer churro batter into large-sized bowl. Use an electric mixer on the low setting to beat for one minute to cool it down. Beat in the egg. Transfer the batter to a pastry bag with a large star-shaped tip.

You'll be cooking four batches of churros. Squeeze 3"-4" lengths of the batter in oil. Use scissors to snip apart as they come out. Fry for about four minutes, till golden brown. Transfer to wire rack sitting on paper towels.

In large mixing bowl, combine last 1/2 cup of sugar with cinnamon. When you can handle the churros, toss them in the sugar-cinnamon mixture. Serve with caramel-chocolate dipping sauce.

26 – Valentine's Day Iced Cake

This tasty cake is easy to prepare, and the icing is sublime. I make it nearly every Valentine's Day.

Makes 16 Servings

Cooking + Prep Time: 55 minutes + 2 hours cooling time

Ingredients:

- 2 cups of sugar, granulated
- 1 cup of softened butter, unsalted
- 4 beaten eggs, large
- 1 tbsp. of vanilla extract, pure
- 1 tsp. of baking powder
- 2 tsp. of baking powder
- 3 cups of flour, all-purpose
- 2 cups of milk, whole
- Icing, prepared

Instructions:

Preheat the oven to 350F. Grease one round 8" pan and one 8" square baking pan.

Beat the sugar and a cup of butter in medium bowl using electric mixer till smooth and creamy. Mix the eggs and vanilla extract into the buttery mixture. Stir baking soda and baking powder in buttery mixture till barely combined.

Stir a cup of flour in buttery mixture till just barely combined. Add 2/3 cup of milk. Combine thoroughly. Continue to alternate adding a cup of flour & 2/3 cup of milk till you have used all flour & milk. Mix till you have a smooth batter. Pour into two pans prepared in step 1.

Bake in 350F oven for 30-40 minutes, till you can insert toothpicks in middle of cakes and have them come back clean. Allow the cakes to completely cool for two hours or longer, then remove cakes from pans.

Slice the round cake into halves. Lay square cake on work surface, resembling the shape of a diamond. Lay one round 1/2 cake on top right side of diamond and one on top left side, creating the shape of a heart on the top. Ice the cake and serve.

27 – Valentine Brownies

These brownies are made in the shapes of hearts to say "Love You" on Valentine's Day or any day. They're chocolaty good and SO sweet.

Makes 16 Servings

Cooking + Prep Time: 45 minutes

Ingredients:

- 3/4 cup of butter, unsalted
- 4 oz. of chocolate, unsweetened
- 4 oz. of chocolate, semi-sweet
- 1/2 cup of flour, all-purpose
- 1/2 cup of cocoa, unsweetened
- 1/2 tsp. of salt, kosher
- 6 eggs, large
- 1 cup of sugar, granulated
- 1 cup of sugar, brown, packed
- 2 tsp. of vanilla extract, pure

Instructions:

Preheat the oven to 350F. Line a 13" x 9" pan using aluminum foil and grease lightly.

In medium pan, melt and stir the butter and both types of chocolate over low heat. Remove from the heat.

In a medium bowl, whisk cocoa, flour & salt together. In larger bowl, using mixer on the high setting, beat the eggs till blended well. Add sugars gradually and beat for 10-12 minutes, till volume has tripled.

Fold in the vanilla and chocolate mixture, then the flour mixture and pour batter into the pan. Bake in 350F oven for 28-30 minutes, till you can insert a toothpick near middle and have it come back nearly clean.

Once brownies have cooled, cut them into heart shapes. Serve.

28 – Rhubarb & Strawberry Shortbread Bars

These rhubarb & strawberry bars will be the perfect finish to a holiday dinner. You can use frozen or fresh rhubarb.

Makes 16 Servings

Cooking + Prep Time: 1 hour & 35 minutes + 2 hours or longer chilling time

Ingredients:

- 1 & 1/2 cups of sliced rhubarb, frozen or fresh
- 1 cup of fresh, sliced strawberries + extra for garnishing
- 1/2 cup + 1/3 cup of sugar, granulated
- 3 tbsp. of sugar, powdered
- 1/2 tsp. of salt, kosher
- 1 cup + 3 tbsp. of flour, all-purpose
- 1/2 cup of cubed, cold butter, unsalted
- 2 whole eggs, large
- 2 egg yolks, large
- 1 tbsp. of lemon zest, fresh
- 5 drops of food coloring, red

Instructions:

Preheat the oven to 350F. Line 9" x 9" pan using baking paper.

Combine the rhubarb with strawberries, 1/2 cup of granulated sugar & 1/4 cup of water in medium pan. Bring to boil. Cook two to four minutes, till fruit has softened and has started breaking down. Allow to cool.

Pulse powdered sugar, 1 cup of flour and kosher salt in food processor till combined, four or five times. Add the butter. Pulse till it forms coarse meal, 10-12 times. Then, firmly press in bottom of pan. Bake in 350F oven for 15-20 minutes, till edges are golden. Cool on wire rack.

Puree the rhubarb and strawberry mixture in food processor till quite smooth, a minute or so. Add the eggs, yolks, lemon zest & 1/3 cup of granulated sugar. Process for 15-20 seconds, till smooth. Add the food coloring & 3 tbsp. of flour. Pulse till just smooth and pour it over the crust.

Bake for 25-30 minutes till set. Completely cool on wire rack. Chill for two hours or longer and cut in squares. Use sliced strawberries to garnish and serve.

29 – Red Velvet Valentine Cookies

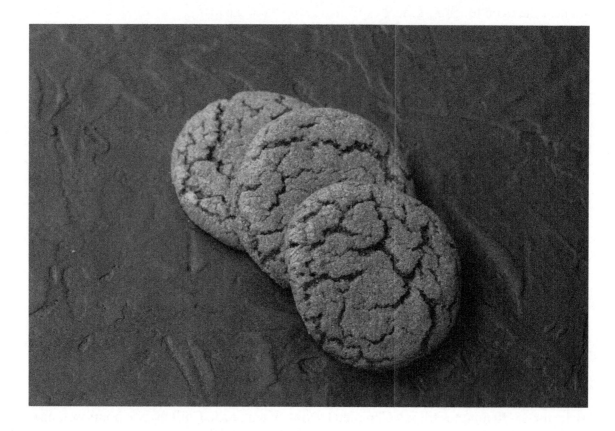

This is a new spin on everyday chocolate chip cookies. They are a vibrant red in color, studded using chocolate chips. They're like mini red velvet cakes.

Makes 30 Servings

Cooking + Prep Time: 50 minutes

Ingredients:

- 2 cups of flour, all-purpose
- 1/2 cup of cocoa powder, unsweetened
- 1 tsp. of salt, kosher
- 1 tsp. of baking soda
- 2 sticks of room temperature butter, unsalted
- 3/4 cup of brown sugar, packed
- 1/2 cup of sugar, granulated
- 1 egg, large
- 1 tsp. of food coloring gel paste, red
- 2 tsp. of vanilla extract, pure
- 1 x 12-oz. pkg. of chocolate chips, semi-sweet

Instructions:

Heat the oven to 350F. Line cookie sheets with baking paper.

In large mixing bowl, whisk flour, cocoa, salt & baking soda together.

Use electric mixer set on med. speed to beat together the butter & both sugars till combined. Then, add the egg, vanilla and food coloring. Mix till barely combined.

Reduce speed of mixer down to low. Add flour mixture till barely combined. Fold in the chocolate chips.

Scoop spoons full of the dough on cookie sheets with 1 & 1/2 inches between them.

Bake the cookies for 9-12 minutes, rotating pans when halfway done, till edges are dark.

Allow cookies to cool on the pans for five minutes. Slide baking paper and cookies onto a wire rack. Let them cool for five minutes or more. Serve.

30 – Pistachio & Raspberry Semifreddo

This creamy and rich dessert is perfect for Valentine's Day. It's something above and beyond the typical strawberries with chocolate.

Makes 6 Servings

Cooking + Prep Time: 45 minutes + 4 hours freezing time

Ingredients:

- 1/4 cup of sour cream, light
- 1/2 cup of sugar, powdered
- 1 cup of cream, heavy
- 1/4 cup of chopped pistachios, unsalted
- 2 pints of raspberries, fresh
- 1 tbsp. of lemon juice, fresh
- 1 tbsp. of honey, pure
- 2 tbsp. of mint leaves, fresh

Instructions:

Line 8" x 4" loaf pan using cling wrap. Leave it overhanging on all sides.

In large bowl, beat the sour cream with electric mixer on med. speed for one minute or so, till smooth. Add the sugar & combine by beating. Reduce speed of mixer down to low setting. Beat in the cream gradually. Increase the speed back up to medium. Beat for two to three minutes, till mixture forms stiff peaks.

Fold in 1 pint of raspberries and pistachios. Transfer batter to pan prepared above. Freeze for four hours or longer, till it sets.

Whisk lemon juice & honey together in medium bowl till they have dissolved. Then, add second pint of raspberries & combine by tossing. Allow mixture to sit, while occasionally tossing, for 18-20 minutes. Invert onto large platter. Discard the cling wrap. Top with mint leaves and raspberries and serve.

Conclusion

This Happy Valentine's Day cookbook has shown you…

How to use different ingredients to affect unique tastes in festive winter dishes.

How can you include Valentine's Day recipes in your home repertoire?

You can…

Make chocolate & ice cream waffles & Nutella & strawberry crepes, which you may not have heard of before. They are just as mouthwatering tasty as they sound.

Cook soups and stews, which are widely served for Valentine's Day. Find ingredients in meat & produce or frozen food sections of your local grocery stores.

Enjoy making delectable seafood dishes of winter, including salmon and shrimp. Fish is a mainstay in their recipes year-round, and there are SO many ways to make it great.

Make dishes using potatoes and pasta in Valentine's Day recipes. There is something about them that delectably makes them more comforting.

Make all kinds of desserts like red velvet cupcakes and pistachio & raspberry semifreddo, which will surely tempt anyone with a sweet tooth.

Enjoy the recipes with your partner!

About the Author

Allie Allen developed her passion for the culinary arts at the tender age of five when she would help her mother cook for their large family of 8. Even back then, her family knew this would be more than a hobby for the young Allie and when she graduated from high school, she applied to cooking school in London. It had always been a dream of the young chef to study with some of Europe's best and she made it happen by attending the Chef Academy of London.

After graduation, Allie decided to bring her skills back to North America and open up her own restaurant. After 10 successful years as head chef and owner, she decided to sell her business and pursue other career avenues. This monumental decision led Allie to her true calling, teaching. She also started to write e-books for her students to study at home for practice. She is now the proud author of several e-books and gives private and semi-private cooking lessons to a range of students at all levels of experience.

Stay tuned for more from this dynamic chef and teacher when she releases more informative e-books on cooking and baking in the near future. Her work is infused with stores and anecdotes you will love!

Author's Afterthoughts

I can't tell you how grateful I am that you decided to read my book. My most heartfelt thanks that you took time out of your life to choose my work and I hope you find benefit within these pages.

There are so many books available today that offer similar content so that makes it even more humbling that you decided to buying mine.

Tell me what you thought! I am eager to hear your opinion and ideas on what you read as are others who are looking for a good book to buy. Leave a review on Amazon.com so others can benefit from your wisdom!

With much thanks,

Allie Allen

Printed in Great Britain
by Amazon

26057679R00051